Face to face

Churches Together in Britain and Ireland
2 Paris Garden
London SE1 8ND

info@ctbi.org.uk or (team)@ctbi.org.uk
www.ctbi.org.uk

ISBN 0 85169 283 4

Published 2003 by Churches Together in Britain and Ireland
Produced by Church House Publishing
Copyright © Churches Together in Britain and Ireland

Further copies available from CTBI Publications,
31 Great Smith Street, London SW1P 3BN

Tel: +44 (0)20 7898 1300
Fax: +44 (0)20 7898 1305

Cover designed by Church House Publishing

Printed in England by Biddles Ltd,
Guildford and King's Lynn

Face to face

Growing into the image and likeness of God

A study and discussion course for use during Lent 2004 and at other times

Edited by Yvonne Craig

bible society making the bible heard

CHURCHES TOGETHER
IN BRITAIN AND IRELAND

Commendation by Presidents of Churches Together in Britain and Ireland and Bible Society

The Lent Course for 2004 is a very special one because it has been prepared jointly by CTBI and representatives of Bible Society. For nearly twenty years CTBI and its predecessor body have been preparing Lent courses every two years which have been widely used by ecumenical groups throughout these islands. But the year 2004 marks the bicentenary of Bible Society and it is a great privilege for CTBI to share in this joint production for the 200th Anniversary. In the light of this, it is particularly appropriate that the 2004 course is based more firmly on a particular biblical text than has happened before.

Since 1996 CTBI has been following the theme of 'Growing into the Image of God' by means of a number of consultations and reflections upon them. Basing the Lent course on sections of the opening chapters of the Gospel according to St Luke is a very creative way of approaching our call to grow into the image and likeness of God. We are helped to do so by reflecting on the Gospel of Jesus, 'the image of the invisible God'. As we seek to be more like Christ so we grow to be more like God. This is a vocation not only for the individual but also for the church community and ultimately, through our witness, for the whole of humanity.

As Presidents of CTBI and of Bible Society, we are happy to commend this course for use in Lent 2004 and at other times of the year. We trust that it will prove an inspiration to many and will encourage us all in our pilgrimage together as the people of God, the community of the Church, a sign and pledge of God's love to the world.

For CTBI

Most Revd Mario Conti   Revd David Kerr   Revd Nezlin Sterling

Most Revd and Rt Hon. David Hope   Sister Eluned Williams

For Bible Society

James Catford
Chief Executive, Bible Society

Most Revd Vincent Nichols
Roman Catholic Vice-President

A special co-operation for a special year

Planning for CTBI Lent Courses begins some years before they are actually published. It was at the very beginning of the new millennium that a suggestion was first made that the proposed course for 2004 on our 'being made in the image of God' should be prepared in co-operation with Bible Society and published as one way of marking its bicentenary in 2004. A writing group decided to base the exploration of the theme in a particular Bible text – namely the first chapters of the Gospel according to St Luke.

It was the unanimous decision of the preparatory group to do this – and one made with considerable enthusiasm. We hope that this will please those people who requested more biblical material on the evaluation forms sent back after using earlier Lent courses and that it will offer those who prefer to work from the basis of experience an opportunity to try another method of Bible study.

Within the course booklet, parts of the biblical text have been quoted in full. Normally CTBI would use texts from the New Revised Standard Version which has widespread acceptance in ecumenical circles. For 2004, however, we are using one of the translations published by Bible Society. We chose to use the Good News Bible – Version 2, which, like the New Revised Standard Version, uses inclusive language. We hope that groups will enjoy the freshness of this translation.

There is another innovation. From the middle of September 2003 if you visit our web site (www.Lent2004.org.uk) you will find suggestions for taking children and young people on a similar journey to the one in this book; plus material for Sunday worship (including sermon notes and Welsh language material) and other resources. You can also tell us about your experiences and ideas and register to receive email updates during Lent 2004. These will include our responses to your feedback and suggestions for bringing any significant breaking news stories into the course.

Since 1996 CTBI has been considering what our calling to grow into the image of God really means. This Lent course is one of the outcomes. The wonder of our human life is that we have this freedom and power to develop in the image of God and in this we rejoice.

From glory to glory advancing we praise you, O Lord.

Jean Mayland,

Co-ordinating Secretary for Church Life,

Churches Together in Britain and Ireland

Contents

Face to face is a three-for-the price-of-one book:

Section 1

Getting the best out of your time together

1. Thinking ahead

2. Why learn in this way?

3. What could we do?

4. How do we use our time together?

5. Ways to ensure no one comes

A flame means you have found a page designed to help you get the best out of your time together.

Section 2

Studying Luke chapters 3 and 4

1. In whose image?

2. Belonging to what?

3. Who is Jesus?

4. Facing our own image

5. Hope – living the image

These pages have a strip down the side showing the number of the session.

Section 3

The image and likeness of God

Six short theological papers designed to deepen your study of the text. These pages are optional and not part of the main course.

1. The image of God in the Bible

2. A fall or a failure to climb?

3. Image and identity

4. The image and likeness of God

5. Male and female in the image of God

6. Excluded from the image

You can identify them by the frame which surrounds them.

Getting the best out of your time together

Section

Thinking ahead

- A good group size is 6–10. If more people want to join, it may be wise to make another group.

- Sometimes you are asked to divide into twos or threes. Two groups in a room can be tricky. If there's more than one group in a room it's important to sit near enough to hear everybody in your group without disturbing the rest.

- Each meeting is designed to last an hour and a half. You may wish to add extra time for a cup of tea or coffee.

- You are likely to get more from *Face to Face* if everyone has a copy. Some paper and something to write with would be useful.

- Arrange the seats in the room so that, as far as possible, everyone can see everyone else.

- Make sure there is at least one Bible handy, as you may want to look up different translations or passages.

- Any new people need at least to hear everyone's name.

Before the meeting

- Read the Bible passage to be studied.

- Read the section on how to get the best out of your group.

- Don't be afraid to select some activities and not others. You don't have to do everything. Some groups like variety, some like to keep to a plan.

- Groups work at different speeds, but check things out with the group. If you take too long at the beginning you may have to leave out a later section which someone is looking forward to as the highlight of the session.

- Remember there are no right or wrong answers to some of the questions. Don't feel guilty if there is disagreement. All our knowledge of God is partial and the wisest minds in the Christian tradition have disagreed.

Ending

- If it looks as though the meeting is going to run on past the time it was supposed to end, say so, say by how much and then stick to the new deadline. If the meeting rambles on, some people may not come back.

- From time to time ask people how the meeting has gone.

- Don't be tempted to say 'We'll do that next week' with the left-overs. Better to start afresh. If the issue is really important it will come up again in a different guise.

- Make sure everyone is clear about when and where the next meeting is to be held.

Optional extra

Suggest that the group notes down any important things that have been said or done, either at the meeting or at home. This is not the same as writing minutes! It could be a different person each week who'd like to record something which particularly struck them. Or you may have someone who likes to draw or do a collage.

Why learn in this way?

We have tried to provide variety within each session and the whole course because…

> …research has shown that people learn in different ways. Some learn best by doing things, but they may be sitting next to someone who is reflective and needs time to think carefully about a subject from different angles. Some need to be sure that the learning has a practical and useful outcome before they are committed to it, while others will only enter a subject deeply if convinced by data and carefully reasoned argument.

We all need to 'unlearn'. …

> …this may mean letting go of attitudes and prejudices which are precious to us and in which over a lifetime we may have invested a great deal. Also, though we may be confident in handling ideas, we may feel uncomfortable with learning which involves feelings or action. We can know a great deal; we can be highly skilled at many things, but if our attitude is wrong, all these things are as nothing.

We are primarily disciples in the world…

> …learning means relating faith and Christ's teaching to everyday experiences. It means taking seriously our deep desire to grow into the full measure of the stature of Christ.

We believe we all have life experience and faith stories to share…

> …all teachers are still learners and all learners have something to teach.

What could we do?

We could work…

Alone You may need time to think, to think beyond your first response. In silence it is easier to reflect on what you have just heard.

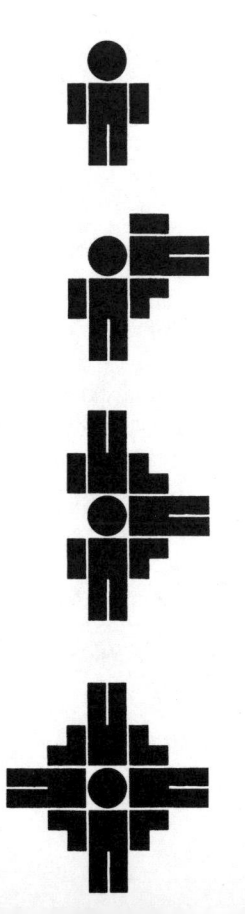

In pairs or triplets This is a place to try out ideas with someone before talking in front of the whole group. Different pairs give you the chance to get to listen to everyone in the group.

In small groups By dividing the group in half, for example, you get twice as much 'air time' as in the whole group. It's a chance to experience a variety of opinions and to go deeper into some issues.

In the whole group This is the pattern many of us are used to. One advantage is that it allows quieter members to be just that, to reflect but not be pressed into a 'public' statement. It can also draw in the expertise of everyone who wishes to contribute. But time is often short, members may not listen to one another so that groups jump from topic to topic and individuals may go off on their own journey.

How do we use our time together?

To Read

It is often wise to ask someone to read the Bible passage aloud to avoid the problem of people reading at different speeds and to make sure that anyone with poor reading or language skills hears the text.

To Do

Each exercise has its guidelines. Remember that they are only suggestions.

To Pray

What is important is to pray about what the group is working on. How you pray is up to the group: we have suggested prayers for you to use; space for silent prayer; hymns or spontaneous prayer spoken aloud. We may need to remind ourselves that this is one place where we can unknowingly crash around assuming that other people's traditions are like our own.

To Ponder

Read the text out loud and leave silence and space for reflection.

To Prepare

Some weeks we suggest ways in which you need to prepare for the next session.

Ways to ensure no one comes

- Avoid all disagreement.
- Assume everyone knows everyone.
- Let the meeting run way past its agreed ending time.
- Allow one person to do all the talking/reading aloud etc.
- Make sure the meeting room is uncomfortably cold or hot.
- Press shy members for spur of the moment opinions and prayers.
- Assume everyone knows where the meeting place is and how to get there.
- Start late so that those who made a huge effort to be on time wait for the others.
- Allow two or three people to conduct an argument which dominates the meeting and doesn't interest anyone else.

If anything else prevented you from going on with your group, write to us or put a message on the web site so that we can put in a warning next time.

Studying Luke chapters 3 and 4

Section

2

Session 1   In whose image?

Welcome (10 minutes)

As this is the first meeting, take a few minutes to introduce yourselves or catch up on news if you know each other.

To Pray

We begin with the Course Prayer which we will use each week and which you might like to use between meetings.

God of love,
God of courage,
God who calls,
meet us face to face on our Lenten journey.
Speak to us through the people whom Jesus met in Galilee and Jordan.
Give us the love and courage to grow into your image
and inspire us so to live
that others may see in us the reflection of your glory.
We ask this in the name of Jesus Christ your Son. Amen

1. The word of God came to John son of Zechariah

(30 minutes)

We begin with Luke's story about a particular person responding to God's call in a particular place and time. We shall read it in three sections, stopping each time to ponder the meaning.

To Read

It was the fifteenth year of the rule of the Emperor Tiberius; Pontius Pilate was Governor of Judea, Herod was ruler of Galilee, and his brother Philip was ruler of the territory of Iturea and Trachonitis; Lysanias was ruler of Abilene, and Annas and Caiaphas were high priests. At that time the word of God came to John son of Zechariah in the desert. (Luke 3.1-2)

The story of Zechariah's son is placed in real time and in a historical situation. Luke names the Roman authorities: the Emperor and the governor of Judea and their allies Herod and his brother Philip. This places the story in the late twenties AD, the fifteenth year of Tiberius, possibly AD 28–29. Rome, the city and its culture, is the centre of the Roman world. Herod and Philip have the power to rule their respective regions because Rome says so. Rome even decides who the local religious leaders will be – in this case Annas and Caiaphas.

But we know that John the Baptizer is seen in three contrasting ways:

- To the Romans, John comes from an insignificant people living in a region on the edge of their Empire.
- On the other hand the Jews do not see themselves as insignificant at all, as we shall see in Session 2.
- In this passage Luke takes a third view. He tells us that John, the son of Zechariah and Elizabeth, is God's chosen messenger. The message is a surprise and the passage will go on to say that it is for everyone.

Before we discuss Luke's words, we are going to consider three short readings from different places and centuries describing how every human being is unique and precious. We believe that each of us
is wonderfully created in God's image and yet more wonderfully restored through the Son Jesus Christ. We have a lifetime to explore what that means.

You are the one who put me together inside my mother's body, and I praise you because of the wonderful way you created me. Everything you do is marvellous! Of this I have no doubt. Nothing about me is hidden from you! I was secretly woven together deep in the earth below, but with your own eyes you saw my body being formed.
(Psalm 139.13-16)

The glory of God is a human being fully alive.
(St Irenaeus, Theologian and Bishop of Lyons, c. 130–200)

The artist Marc Quinn, born in 1964 in London, made eight nude, life-size marble statues which were displayed at the Victoria and Albert Museum in 2000 in a hall among many familiar classical sculptures like Canova's The Three Graces. His figures were of four women and four men, each deprived of one or more limbs by birth, illness or accident.

Quinn used the sitters' names, emphasizing that the statues represent individuals not mythological figures. Walking around the sculpture hall I felt the furniture in my mind being shifted and classical ideas of beauty and heroism and perfection being displaced by something more to God's way of thinking.
(Yvonne Craig, 2003)

To Do

Discuss in pairs or triplets: Does anything you have read in this session so far throw any light on what it means to be made in the image of God?

In the group: Share any phrase or thought that has struck you. Be brief. There'll be a chance to talk more later.

2. In the desert (20 minutes)

To Read

> At that time the word of God came to John son of Zechariah in the desert. So John went throughout the whole territory of the River Jordan, preaching, 'Turn away from your sins and be baptized, and God will forgive your sins.' As it is written in the book of the prophet Isaiah: 'Someone is shouting in the desert: "Get the road ready for the Lord; make a straight path for him to travel!"' (Luke 3.2-4)

Here Luke is describing John's experience in the desert or wilderness, waiting and listening, hoping that God will speak and give him a message for the world. In the fourth session we'll be learning something about Jesus' experience of a real wilderness.

Here John, like Jesus, chose to go into the wilderness. Sometimes, however, we feel that's where we are but we did not choose it – the wilderness visits us without asking our permission. Then we are using 'wilderness' to mean a special time when things are hard and normal life seems far away. Often it is a crisis which changes us, touches our soul and startles it. Perhaps it comes in one decisive moment, after which we know life will never be the same. Or it may creep up on us slowly. It can help us imagine unexpected ways of growing into the image of God here and now.

To Do

Choose between these two sets of questions. The second is particularly useful if the group members are well known to each other.

1. Does your group have people with different traditions for setting aside time for God? What are they? If anyone has been on a retreat or to a convention recently, what difference would it have made if you hadn't gone?

2. Sometimes we are tried and tested almost beyond endurance. If you've experienced anything like that, who or what kept you going? Other people, memories, sacraments, silence, music, going for walks, something you read?

3. The whole human race will see God's salvation (30 minutes)

To Ponder

> *Get the road ready for the Lord; make a straight path for him to travel! Every valley must be filled up, every hill and mountain levelled off. The winding roads must be made straight, and the rough paths made smooth. The whole human race will see God's salvation.* (Luke 3. 5-6)

- **John proclaims good news:** although the valleys of life may be too low and mountains of circumstances may be too high, God is with us, God is the Way Maker. We live in a world of make-overs: homes and gardens are refashioned on TV, surgery and medicines give a patient new life, infertile couples become parents, workers are made redundant, green land is re-zoned for housing, divorce means a new start with or without a partner, refugees become citizens, grants to re-train may mean a new job.

- **John proclaims a new message:** he is urging us to turn from what is not worth gaining – from the lure of make-overs which may leave us dry and unsatisfied – to our true goal, which we can never quite reach.

- **John proclaims 'God's salvation':** the world is a vast bundle of opportunities which Jesus offers, a fullness of experience of which we had long since despaired. Everyone shall see the salvation of God. And Jesus really means everyone. We do not earn it by being good.

God took a risk in creation. His purpose is always threatened when we misuse or waste our human powers. What trips us up? Why don't we get the message? Is it because we deny the need for forgiveness?

11

Forgiveness gives us

>the energy which saves us from decay,
>and the courage that overcomes our fear.
>It is an opportunity grasped
>a call answered
>a responsibility shouldered.

Goodness means

>other people find sympathy where they
>expected vindictiveness,
>concern when they expected indifference,
>generosity where they expected retribution.

It forces us out of our private world towards our neighbours where we may become a symbol of hope.

To Do

In the group: Drawing on your own experience, choose a phrase about forgiveness or goodness which rings most true. First, go round the group briefly so that everyone who wants to can share their phrase. Then do the same with a phrase which means the least to you, either because its meaning isn't clear or because it doesn't ring true to your experience of life. Then if there's time share with others more fully why the words mean something to you.

Alone: Take some time during the coming week to think about the phrases you chose. Is there any way they could be pointing you to a new understanding of what it means to grow in the image of God?

To Pray (10 minutes)

We suggest prayers for each of the sessions but you may prefer to use your own prayers, to sing, or to use all or some of the time remaining in silent worship.

>*Almighty God, who wonderfully created us in your own image*
>*and yet more wonderfully restored us*
>*through your Son Jesus Christ:*
>*grant that, as he came to share in our humanity,*
>*so we may share the life of his divinity;*
>*who is alive and reigns with you,*
>*in the unity of the Holy Spirit,*
>*one God, now and for ever.*
>*Amen*

(Collect for Christmas 1)

>*Praise to you, O Christ, king of eternal glory!*
>*Blessed are those who, with a noble and generous heart,*
>*take the word of God to themselves*
>*and yield a harvest through their perseverance.*
>*Praise to you, O Christ, king of eternal glory!*
>*Lord, may everything we do this week*
>*begin with your inspiration,*
>*continue with your help*
>*and reach perfection under your guidance.*
>*Amen*

To Prepare for the next session

Think about significant times and events in the history of your church, neighbourhood or other communities to which you belong.

The group will need:

- Pieces of card in the shape of bricks. Write words on some of them to suggest things which divide people: self interest, greed, fear of foreigners, loyalty to a group, prejudice, fear of being rejected. Leave others blank for people to write their own words.
- A small table or floor space on which to put the cards.
- A small cross to place on the table. It could be a crucifix, a pendant, a post card, an icon or anything to remind us of Jesus Christ.
- Some quiet and reflective music and the means to play it.

Session 2   Belonging to what?

To Pray

God of love,
God of courage,
God who calls,
meet us face to face on our Lenten journey.
Speak to us through the people whom Jesus met in Galilee and Jordan.
Give us the love and courage to grow into your image
and inspire us so to live
that others may see in us the reflection of your glory.
We ask this in the name of Jesus Christ your Son. Amen

1. Bringing history alive (20 minutes)

To Read

Last week we read the story of John the Baptist, how he preached about the coming of Jesus, the bearer of the good news of God's salvation. We told each other some of our own personal stories of faith in God. This week we shall look at a wider picture – the story of the communities and nations from which we come. Unfortunately, the very thing which unites some can make others feel that they do not belong. John's replies in the passage we shall read show that in God's eyes no one is excluded, although they can exclude themselves. We are who we are today because of our history, the history of the communities: our families, churches, nation, language, customs and culture. An old Russian proverb puts it like this:

If you live in the past you lose an eye.
But if you forget the past you go completely blind.

The trouble is that many of us had to learn someone else's history rather than our own. It may have been about powerful families and leaders; it may have been a foreign nation's history. Perhaps there are people in your group from different nations and communities. We gradually discover that all history is taught from a particular point of view. Usually those who win the battle write the history of the war. 'We' were the goodies, 'they' were the baddies. History, biased or not, has shaped us. To get a fuller picture we need the help of our families, friends, church and neighbourhood. Listening to their stories deepens our understanding of the past. Then we are freer to appreciate the present and move on in our journey of life and faith.

To Do

In pairs or triplets: Make a list of what you feel are the important times and events in the history of your local community. Just use headings – or even a quick drawing – as you think of things. There will be time for discussion in the group.

In the group: Share your lists and ask what makes us feel that we belong (or do not belong) to the communities in which we live? How do we feel about talking about the past?

2. To belong or not to belong? (25 minutes)

To Read

Crowds of people came out to John to be baptized by him. 'You snakes!' he said to them. 'Who told you that you could escape from the punishment God is about to send? Do those things that will show that you have turned from your sins. And don't start saying among yourselves that Abraham is your ancestor. I tell you that God can take these stones and make descendants for Abraham! The axe is ready to cut down the trees at the roots; every tree that does not bear good fruit will be cut down and thrown in the fire.' The people asked him, 'What are we to do, then?' He answered, 'Whoever has two shirts must give one to the man who has none, and whoever has food must share it.' Some tax collectors came to be baptized, and they asked him, 'Teacher, what are we to do?' 'Don't collect more than is legal,' he told them. Some soldiers also asked him, 'What about us? What are we to do?' He said to them, 'Don't take money from anyone by force or accuse anyone falsely. Be content with your pay.' (Luke 3.7-14)

In many ways this passage is about people who feel that they belong to one another. The crowd was probably a fairly typical Jewish group. Most of them came to John with the belief that, simply because they were Jewish, they automatically had a special relationship with God.

For most Jews of that time, being a descendant of Abraham and belonging to the Jewish faith were one and the same thing. Biology, politics and religion went together. Yet there were others in the crowd, people like the tax collectors, who had sided with the Romans and their occupying troops. They believed it was possible to be both Jewish and loyal to Rome. Indeed, some Roman soldiers were present in the crowd in front of John.

But John challenges everyone. What does it mean to belong? He tells them that their understanding of 'belonging' to God is too narrow. In answers to the three questions presented to him, John highlights what it really means to be a member of a nation and to belong to the 'people of God'.

To Do

Our history can 'cement' or 'knit' us together as a community and as a nation. But what keeps people out? There are ancient biblical images of barriers and walls, bricks or stones, which can separate people and a nation. In a moment you will be given a 'brick' or two. Some will have words on them describing what might divide us, others will be blank.

In the group: Some people have a strong sense of belonging to a nation or community, others do not. What, if anything, is good about belonging? What might be dangerous? Nations and groups have to have rules about who belongs. Some of the most difficult decisions centre on who to exclude. Unruly children from school, for example? Asylum seekers? Some criminals – but which ones?

Alone: What unites or divides us? In silence, write on a blank brick your own words to describe what it feels like to belong to your nation or your community, or to be excluded. Or you may like to imagine how it is for other people. When you are ready, place the bricks on a table or floor space around a small cross to form a makeshift wall. We'll use them in the closing worship.

3. Let nothing separate us (30 minutes)

To Read

Three questions were put to John the Baptist in today's Bible passage:

- The first came from the crowd who thought they belonged simply because they were 'children of Abraham'.
- A second question came from the despised tax collectors who were shunned by 'decent society'.
- Soldiers from the occupying Roman army asked the third question.

Each group asked, in effect, 'What does it mean to belong?' John's replies show that nothing is more important than knowing that we are all made in the image of God, along with every other human being. 'Living in the image of God' is not about belonging to a certain group or nation. It is about

- living with integrity
- being open to the stranger
- being generous with our possessions
- and just in our actions.

To Do

In the group: Grand words have to be made to work in our nation and local communities. What questions might the crowd shout out today? What questions would you ask?

- Would they be about money: 'Why are some people paid so much and others so little?'
- Or health: 'With whom do we share our National Health Service?'
- Or age: 'Why are some old people neglected?'

John was asked 'What must we do to belong?' The answers given probably meant fundamental change in the questioners' lives if they wanted to bring down a barrier between them and God. Name a change which would help someone belong. We cannot begin to answer these things now but we can get back to listening to what God says about the value of every human being.

4. Reflection and worship (15 minutes)

To Ponder

In a few minutes we shall be thinking about what we might do in our lives to remove barriers. There will then be an opportunity to remove one or more bricks from the wall that surrounds the cross or blocks it off from us. But before that we are going to listen to Jean Vanier reflecting on what community and belonging might be. He is the founder of the L'Arche communities, which offer those with disability and those who share their lives a place where they can grow and belong. Being together with others is not always easy. We are all fallen, broken people.

Jean Vanier says:

> *The ideal community, in which there is no rivalry and each one finds his or her place, is not something that can be achieved once and for all. It requires daily struggle. Difficulties in relationships, jealousies, anger and fear all spring up very quickly in community life. One starts to ignore certain people. People can be living together in a house and yet pass one another like ships in the night...*

Community living and the search for unity demand a constant effort to be attentive to and respectful of others, especially those whom we find less agreeable. They demand an effort to accept differences and to live forgiveness daily.

To Pray

You may want to play music while those who wish to are invited to come to the cross and take one of the bricks away. They may like to read the following phrase aloud while doing this:

We pray that in our living and belonging . . . (insert the words on the brick here) . . . may never separate us from your love and from one another.

After everyone has had the chance to take a brick away, the rest of the bricks should be removed to another place.

After some quiet reflection, read out the following prayer:

Heart-stopping God, we give you thanks
for the times when we have caught a glimpse of your wonder,
those moments when our breath has been taken away
and our power of understanding has disappeared,
when we have been silenced with the wonder of your power
and the fierceness of your gentleness.

Barrier-breaking God,
we give you thanks
for all those people
who have shown us through their living
a vision of how the world might be,
a way of loving which welcomes all,
a way of living which accepts all,
a way of working which includes all,
a way of being which involves all.

Division-destroying God,
we give you thanks
for all those who have sought to bring light to dark places,
who have struggled to shatter the darkness of disease by healing,
who have chased the shadows of violence with the weapons of peace,
who have nursed rays of hope for all forgotten victims and silent lips.

Today and every day, Lord God,
convince us of your love,
convict us of your challenge,
that we may learn to see around us
a world of possibilities,
a place of opportunity.

And where these do not exist,
challenge us
to begin again to create with you
that kingdom beyond barriers,
where we live as
one people,
one race,
one kingdom
under one love. Amen

Blessing

In leaving may God's voice
whisper love to our ears,
In resting may we hear the peace
of the Spirit spoken,
In quietness may we hear the
walking of Christ's kingdom.

As you go from here
May God hold and guard,
heal and protect you
until in the light of our next
meeting
we may hear the call of God
and listen to love's voice again.
Amen

Session 3 Who is Jesus?

1. Who are we? (20 minutes)

To Pray

Begin your time together before God with prayer (and
perhaps a song of worship), including the course prayer:

God of love,
God of courage,
God who calls,
meet us face to face on our Lenten journey.
Speak to us through the people whom Jesus met in Galilee and Jordan.
Give us the love and courage to grow into your image
and inspire us so to live
that others may see in us the reflection of your glory.
We ask this in the name of Jesus Christ your Son. Amen

To Read

Last week we talked about how communities reflect the
image of God – or fail to do so. In our Bible story, John the
Baptist challenged the people of his community to repent.
We thought about what it means to belong or to be excluded in our
churches, communities and nation. This week's Bible passage has a
familiar story followed by a rather strange list of names. Here we
meet Jesus, God's Son, a particular human being just as we are,
except that he is the one who definitively and finally demonstrated
by his words and actions what God is like. Colossians 1.15 calls
Jesus 'the image of the invisible God'. In him we find clues as to
what it means for us to be made in the image of God.

In looking at Jesus we shall think about
- Something you hoped God would be
- Something you feared God might be or do
- Something you are surprised God is.

We shall spend 20 minutes on each of those ideas but we begin by
reading the first half of Luke 3.15-28 aloud, and the rest silently.

> People's hopes began to rise, and they began to wonder
> whether John perhaps might be the Messiah. So John said to all
> of them, 'I baptize you with water, but someone is coming who
> is much greater than I am. I am not good enough even to untie
> his sandals. He will baptize you with the Holy Spirit and fire.
> He has his winnowing shovel with him, to thresh out all the
> grain and gather the wheat into his barn; but he will burn the
> chaff in a fire that never goes out.' In many different ways John
> preached the Good News to the people and urged them to
> change their ways. But John reprimanded Herod, the governor,
> because he had married Herodias, his brother's wife, and had

done many other evil things. Then Herod did an even worse thing by putting John in prison. After all the people had been baptized, Jesus also was baptized. While he was praying heaven was opened, and the Holy Spirit came down upon him in bodily form like a dove. And a voice came from heaven, 'You are my own dear Son. I am pleased with you.'

Do not read the next part of this passage aloud, but ask group members to look through it quietly themselves.

When Jesus began his work, he was about thirty years old. He was the son, so people thought, of Joseph, who was the son of Heli, the son of Matthat, the son of Levi, the son of Melchi, the son of Jannai, the son of Joseph, the son of Mattathias, the son of Amos, the son of Nahum, the son of Esli, the son of Naggai, the son of Maath, the son of Mattathias, the son of Semein, the son of Josech, the son of Joda, the son of Joanan, the son of Rhesa, the son of Zerubbabel, the son of Shealtiel, the son of Neri, the son of Melchi, the son of Addi, the son of Cosam, the son of Elmadam, the son of Er, the son of Joshua, the son of Eliezer, the son of Jorim, the son of Matthat, the son of Levi, the son of Simeon, the son of Judah, the son of Joseph, the son of Jonam, the son of Eliakim, the son of Melea, the son of Menna, the son of Mattatha, the son of Nathan, the son of David, the son of Jesse, the son of Obed, the son of Boaz, the son of Salmon, the son of Nahshon, the son of Amminadab, the son of

Admin, the son of Arni, the son of Hezron, the son of Perez, the son of Judah, the son of Jacob, the son of Isaac, the son of Abraham, the son of Terah, the son of Nahor, the son of Serug, the son of Reu, the son of Peleg, the son of Eber, the son of Shelah, the son of Cainan, the son of Arphaxad, the son of Shem, the son of Noah, the son of Lamech, the son of Methuselah, the son of Enoch, the son of Jared, the son of Mahalaleel, the son of Kenan, the son of Enosh, the son of Seth, the son of Adam, the son of God.

The genealogy

Genealogy means 'list of ancestors'. Here Jesus is traced back through Joseph to Adam. Some of the names are people whose stories we may know – King David, for example, or Abraham, Isaac, Jacob and Noah. Others make only fairly brief appearances in the Old Testament – Zerubbabel, whose story is found in parts of the books of Ezra, Haggai and Zechariah. Others again are unknown to us. Why does Luke break into his story to insert such a forbidding list of names? It hardly encourages us to read his book, after all.

One of the writers of this course was travelling through the Middle East many years ago when he gave a Gospel to an Arab man, who was at first very reluctant to accept it. When he leafed through it the genealogy of Jesus really interested him. He commented 'This smells of the truth'.

Surnames originated in Europe because there was a need to distinguish between people who bore the same name. One John was the smith, another had red hair, another was the son of a man called James. Enter John Smith, John Redhead, and John Jameson. Children took their father's name (if known) and a woman her husband's name, but this custom is changing.

Again, a member of the writing group can trace his own family tree back to the 1450s. This is important in the Hindu culture from which his family comes. For instance, there is a religious duty to your ancestors (praying for the departed and ensuring that they have reached a good safe place). Also in some traditions marriage is forbidden between people who have a common ancestor within seven generations.

Surnames are extremely important in Hindu culture. Your destiny is written in your name. It determines your caste distinction, shows where you stand in the social order, the dignity that should be afforded to you and what profession you should follow.

The genealogy in Luke's Gospel is all about establishing who Jesus is. In John's Gospel, some Jewish leaders revile Jesus because, as they say, 'we do not know where he comes from' (John 9.29). Luke addresses this question.

Nowadays more and more people trace their family tree. Why do they do it?

2. Something you hoped God would be (20 minutes)

Before the genealogy, Luke's record of Jesus' baptism starts with people wondering if John the Baptist is the Christ or the Messiah. It is not clear how widespread the Jewish expectation of a Messiah was, or how varied were the pictures of what the Messiah might be like. Certainly, some people were looking for God to send them a warrior king like David, who would throw off Roman rule and restore the glories of the Jewish nation. Others may have had more spiritual goals. But they were agreed that the fortunes of God's chosen people were at a low ebb and that a king sent by God would change that, even if they were not certain how. When they saw what John did and said, some wondered if he might be the one they were waiting for.

And then Jesus breaks into the story, a human being with his own particular identity just like us. He is also the image of God in human form. It is important, however, not to link any one human characteristic of Jesus with his divinity. It is not particularly divine to be Jewish, or male, or a carpenter.

To Do

Alone: If you could ask God to do one thing for the world, knowing he would do it, what would you ask? Promote righteousness? Punish evil? Alleviate suffering? Right political wrongs? Is God more concerned with the Church or the world? Write down one thing you hope God would do.

In the group: Do you have different ideas of what God should do? Share your answer.

3. Something you feared God might be or do
(20 minutes)

We are now going to imagine what it would be like to be there when John was baptizing. The meditation below is to be read slowly, leaving space for you to picture the scenes and use your imagination. Your group may like to do this in silence or with quiet music in the background. You may like to close your eyes and relax.

To Do

Imagine that you are one of a group of people who have come to hear John (pause). Picture the scene: John is standing in the river Jordan, preaching to crowds of people on the banks (pause). How much can you see? (pause) What noises are there? (pause)

Smells? (pause) What does it feel like to be there? (pause) Watch as people – ordinary people, some of them your friends and neighbours – wade into the river and are plunged under the water by John (pause). Do you feel embarrassed, impressed, wish you were there? John speaks of a baptism of repentance; what do their faces look like as they come out of the water? (pause) What might they be feeling? (pause) Someone asks John if he is the Messiah. Perhaps John laughs. Certainly he says 'No'. Then he goes on to say: 'I baptize you with water, but someone is coming who is much greater than I am. I am not good enough even to untie his sandals. He will baptize you with the Holy Spirit and fire. He has his winnowing shovel with him, to thresh out all the grain and gather the wheat into his barn; but he will burn the chaff in a fire that never goes out.' As you stand by the river bank, how do you feel when you hear these words? Do you find them confusing? Is it upsetting to hear all that talk about fire and judgement? Or exciting? In silence choose one or two words which express how you feel.

Now come back together as a group and share your thoughts and feelings. Listen carefully to other people's experience. Write down one thing you feared God might be or do.

Baptism in the Holy Spirit

If there is time, you may want to discuss that intriguing phrase 'baptism in the Holy Spirit'.

The meaning of the phrase 'baptism in the Holy Spirit' has been much disputed recently. Some Christians, influenced by Pentecostal traditions, or by charismatic renewal, have seen it as a new experience of God. This might come some time after water baptism, and results in the giving of spiritual gifts, a new infilling of the Holy Spirit, and also in new joy and new commitment in the Christian life. Many have found inspiration and enthusiasm through experiences like this, and much good has been done as a result. Charismatic renewal has given new life to many Christian people and churches, and we should welcome that, and thank God for the good things that have come. Most New Testament scholars, however, do not think that the phrase 'baptism in the Holy Spirit' refers to such an experience when John the Baptist uses it here. Instead, they think that it is linked to the promise that the Spirit will be given when we are baptized in water. This is not to deny the reality of Pentecostal/charismatic experience, of course; only to suggest that it is probably not what John the Baptist is talking about here.

To Ponder

> *After all the people had been baptized, Jesus also was baptized. While he was praying, heaven was opened, and the Holy Spirit came down upon him in bodily form like a dove.*
> *And a voice came from heaven, 'You are my own dear Son. I am pleased with you.'* (Luke 3.22)

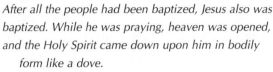

God calling Jesus his Son could mean many things. It might remind us:

● of the full-blown doctrine of the Trinity, seeing this as a reference to the fact that the Jewish man Jesus is God the Son incarnate;

● that the Davidic king was regularly called 'God's son' in the psalms;

● of the way Jesus taught us all to call God 'Father' and see him as a human being who prays here just as we do.

We don't have to decide between these ideas; the story is rich enough to contain them all:

● the baptism of Jesus, with the Father sending the Spirit to the Son, is a classic text used by many churches on Trinity Sunday to illuminate what Christians mean when they talk about one God in three persons;

- equally, the genealogy that follows this text makes the point that Jesus is the son of David, and that this is central to what it meant to be the Messiah;
- Jesus' baptism is the moment when he identifies himself fully with us as a human person among other human persons. It is the moment when he shares our hopes, dreams, desires and aspirations, and also shares our failures and sins (this is a baptism of repentance) until he can do away with them on the cross.

Jesus is the Son of God, however, and so what he does is God-like, and the voice from heaven announces that the Father is pleased with him. Thus we can look at the life of Jesus to find an image of what God is like. Michael Ramsey, a former Archbishop of Canterbury, said 'God is Christlike and in him is no unChristlikeness at all.'

To Do

Look again at what you wrote about what you would like God to be. Can you think of a story in the gospels where Jesus displays those characteristics? Now think of the thing you feared God might be. Does Jesus ever act like this in the gospels? Finally think of a gospel story that you find puzzling, difficult or confusing. Is there something you are surprised God is?

5. Closing reflection and worship (10 minutes)

By now you should have recognized three characteristics displayed by Jesus, who is the image of the invisible God:

- Something you hoped God would be
- Something you feared God might be or do
- Something you are surprised God is

Each member of the group may like to say the following prayer, inserting words from their own lists.

Our God,

we thank you that in the life of Jesus your Son, the true image,

you have revealed to us what you are like.

You fulfil our desires, and we thank you that in him we see that you are………….and that you are not…... more.....

You challenge our assumptions, and we thank you that in him we see that you are………..

You surprise our expectations, and we thank you that in him we see that you are……….

Continue to show us more of who you are, we pray.   Amen.

You may also wish to spend some time praising God for all that he is, particularly for the things we have identified, by focusing on Jesus and his work. Some appropriate worship songs are: 'The Servant King', 'Meekness and majesty', or 'Lord, we lift your name on high'. Each group will no doubt have their favourites. Between the songs, encourage people to offer short prayers thanking God for the things on their lists, or to pray in silence.

To Prepare for the next session

P

The group will need

- A broken or cracked jar, plate, box or vessel of some kind.

- Either a short clip from a recent news programme which could be displayed on a TV screen or a selection of cuttings from a national and/or local newspapers featuring situations of 'brokenness'.

- Blank cards on which to write comments.

Session 4 Facing our own image

1. The temptations of Jesus (20 minutes)

To Pray

God of love,
God of courage,
God who calls,
Meet us face to face on our Lenten journey.
Speak to us through the people whom Jesus met in Galilee and Jordan.
Give us the love and courage to grow into your image
and inspire us so to live
that others may see in us the reflection of your glory.
We ask this in the name of Jesus Christ your Son. Amen

To Read

- In our Bible story last week we looked at Jesus, the bearer of the image of God. We thought about his human family tree and about his baptism as God's Son and Messiah. We told our own stories of what we hope for from God through Jesus.

- This session helps us discover more about growing into the image of God in times of temptation and weakness. Our Bible passage may be a familiar Lenten story to some: Luke's account of the temptations of Jesus. In a few minutes we shall also be reading a shocking passage from a recent novel describing what living and starving alone in a desert might be like. We're not trying to pretend the writer knows exactly what happened to Jesus, but the passage may give us insights into a story which is part of our Christian heritage and which shapes our Christian lives.

- And we use the idea of 'brokenness' to reflect on what the temptation story means in the context of our everyday life.

Jesus returned from the Jordan full of the Holy Spirit and was led by the Spirit into the desert, where he was tempted by the Devil for forty days. In all that time he ate nothing, so that he was hungry when it was over. The Devil said to him, 'If you are God's Son, order this stone to turn into bread.' But Jesus answered, 'The scripture says, "Human beings cannot live on bread alone." ' Then the Devil took him up and showed him in a second all the kingdoms of the world. 'I will give you all this power and all this wealth,' the Devil told him. 'It has all been handed over to me, and I can give it to anyone I choose. All this will be yours, then, if you worship me.' Jesus answered, 'The scripture says, "Worship the Lord your God and serve only him!" ' Then the Devil took him to Jerusalem and set him on the highest point of the Temple, and said to him, 'If you are God's Son, throw yourself down from here. For the scripture says, "God will order his angels to take good care of you." It also says, "They will hold you up with their hands so that not even your feet will be hurt on the stones." ' But Jesus answered, 'The scripture says, "Do not put the Lord your God to the test."' When the Devil finished tempting Jesus in every way, he left him for a while. (Luke 4.1-13)

To Do

For some, this passage suggests a superhuman, flawless image of a Christ who will never, under any circumstance, give in to temptation. Some maintain that these temptations kept on returning to Jesus throughout his life and when he was hanging on the cross. Others believed that Jesus was only tempted to choose evil once, in the desert, and not throughout his life. What it undoubtedly shows is that Jesus would not use his divinity and deny his humanity. He remained true to who he was.

In pairs or triplets: Spend some time thinking what the passage says to you about Jesus. Can you recognize anything of yourself in this story?

2. Experiencing the desert (20 minutes)

To Read

Now we invite you to reflect on the story in a slightly different way. Though Jesus does overcome evil in the desert, he doesn't achieve this without the human struggle of having to come to terms with his own vulnerability. What it might have been like is described by Jim Crace in this extract from his novel *Quarantine*:

No one had said how painful it would be, how first there would be headaches and bad breath, weakness, fainting; or how the coating on the upper surface of his tongue would thicken day by day; or how his tongue would soon become stuck to the upper part of his mouth, held in place by gluey strings of hunger, so that he would mutter to himself or say his prayers as if his palate had been cleft at birth; or how his gums would bleed and his teeth become as loose as date stones.

No one had warned him how quickly he would lose his will to move about, how even lifting up his arms to wipe away the sweat – so much of that, at first, and then none at all – would become a punishing task; how he'd postpone the effort and let the sweat drip off his brow without regard to cleanliness; how cruelly his body would begin to eat itself as his muscles and his liver and his kidneys fought for fuel like squalid, desert boys battling for a piece of wood; how his legs would swell with pus; how his skin would tear and how the wounds would be

*too weak to dress themselves with scabs. No one had said,
there will be stomach pains and cramps, demanding to be
rubbed and soothed like dogs.*

To Do

In the group: How do you react to Jim Crace's word-painting?

Jesus, we are told, was 'hungry' (translated sometimes as
'famished'). Did that include a need for human contact? We all
know what it means to feel pain, to feel abandoned and lonely. Evil
often strikes at times like these. For Christ the challenge would again
be at its sharpest in the Garden of Gethsemane when he asked God
whether he could escape the pain of the cross. Is it a comfort to you
that Christ went through these terrible experiences?

Alone: Write down any words which come to mind and place them
in or on the broken vessel. We will use them in our final prayers.

3. When things are broken (10 minutes)

To Ponder

In pairs or triplets: What does this image make you think of?

Who or what is the string?

Who or what is the strong chain?

Alone: Write down any words which come to mind and place them
in or on the broken vessel. We will use them in our final prayers.

4. Being broken in the world (25 minutes)

Tragedy or illness or disability can strike anyone. Now we are going to look at some news items, national or local, using a short clip from a recent TV programme or items from newspapers.

To Do

In the group: tackle one or more of these questions:

- Who or what is broken by what has happened?

- What does it make you feel?

- What is the cause (if any) of the distress?

- Can you imagine anything good coming either from the event itself or its exposure to the reader or the viewer? This is an increasingly important question in a world which encourages us to watch other people's pain and difficulty, in reality TV for example, or in prying news coverage.

- The opposite of being broken is to be whole. But what is 'wholeness'? Is healing always the answer? Some Christians may feel that their faith should act as a security blanket and that they 'are letting God down' when things go badly. Surely if they prayed more, all would be well? Are they right?

To Pray (15 minutes)

What does 'brokenness' mean to those you know, to those you have read about or even to you in your own life at this time? If you wish, share your concerns briefly with the group. Whether or not you speak, you may wish to write on the cards provided and place them in the broken vessel.

Anyone who wants to is invited to hold the vessel for a few moments. Pray for each other and the concerns on your mind and heart.

You may like to pass the vessel round, either in silence or with some music playing.

Place the vessel back in the centre of the room.

Sitting in a circle with the broken vessel in the centre, say together:

> **We bring you our hopes.**
> **We bring you our wounds.**
> **We bring you our dreams.**
> **We bring you our broken lives.**
> **We offer them all to you.**
> **Touch us and transform us.**
> **Hold us and heal us.**
> **And let your image shine in us.**
> **That the world may see the power of your love. Amen**
>
> (Meg Gilley)

The session ends with the following prayer, which is led by one of the group members.

God of the heights and the depths,
we bring to you
those driven into the desert,
those suffering with difficult decisions
May they choose life.

God of the light and the darkness
we bring to you
those lost in the mist of drugs and drink,
those dazzled by the use of power.
May they choose life.

God of the wild beast and the ministering angel,
we bring to you
those savaged by others' greed,
those exhausted by caring for others.
May they feel your healing touch.

Christ tempted and triumphant,
we bring ourselves to you,
tired of difficult choices,
anxious about the future,
drained by the loss of a loved one.
May we feel your healing touch.

May we feel your healing touch,
know God's presence in all things
and receive the crown of life
through the Holy Spirit of compassion.
Amen

(Kate McIlhagga)

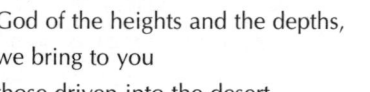

To prepare for the next session

The group will need to decide:

- whether or not it is going to take up the suggestion to use tealights (or other small candles) in the closing worship. If so, someone will need to bring them plus some matches.

- which of the suggested five prayers are going to be used, including the option of using them all.

You will need to provide:

- some quiet music and a means to play it;
- a table or cloth on the floor in the centre of the room.

In addition each member will need to bring:

- an object or picture or perhaps something written which is a symbol of what she or he has learned in this course.

Session 5 Hope – living the image

1. Introduction (10 minutes)

Today's session is about hope.

- Jesus returns to Nazareth filled with the power of the Spirit after his time in the wilderness.

- We also come to the end of Lent and look forward with hope as we recognize the work of God in Christ, who is the image of God.

- This is our hope: to bring hope to others in the power of the Spirit.

We begin with a story, told in new ways as well as in the old way. Then we will explore that story:

- What does it tell us not only about the characters then but about ourselves now?

- What does it tell us about the realities and the challenges of being made in the image of God?

- Why do we dare to have hope for the world?

This session is the last in the series. It is important to set aside a good stretch of time at the end for closing worship.

In this worship you will have an opportunity to gather up the story of your time together by sharing the contributions people have brought along, as invited last week, and by bringing today's session to a close in prayer.

To Pray

As well as the course prayer you may wish to include the Lord's Prayer here, and one or two spontaneous prayers, or silence, as appropriate for the group.

God of love
God of courage,
God who calls,
Meet us face to face on our Lenten journey.
Speak to us through the people whom Jesus met in Galilee and Jordan.
Give us the love and courage to grow into your image
and inspire us so to live
that others may see in us the reflection of your glory.
We ask this in the name of Jesus Christ your Son. Amen

2. The story of Jesus in the synagogue at Nazareth (30 minutes)

To Read

Then Jesus returned to Galilee, and the power of the Holy Spirit was with him. The news about him spread throughout all that territory. He taught in the synagogues and was praised by everyone. Then Jesus went to Nazareth, where he had been brought up, and on the Sabbath he went as usual to the synagogue. He stood up to read the Scriptures and was handed the book of the prophet Isaiah. He unrolled the scroll and found the place where it is written: 'The Spirit of the Lord is upon me, because he has chosen me to bring good news to the poor. He has sent me to proclaim liberty to the captives and recovery of sight to the blind; to set free the oppressed and announce that the time has come when the Lord will save his people.' Jesus rolled up the scroll, gave it back to the attendant, and sat down. All the people in the synagogue had their eyes fixed on him, as he said to them, 'This passage of scripture has come true today, as you heard it being read.' They were all well impressed with him and marvelled at the eloquent words that he spoke. They said, 'Isn't he the son of Joseph?' He said to them, 'I am sure that you will quote this proverb to me, "Doctor, heal yourself." You will also tell me to do here in my home town the same things you heard were done in Capernaum. I tell you this,' Jesus added, 'prophets are never welcomed in their home town. Listen to me: it is true that there were many widows in Israel during the time of Elijah, when there was no rain for three and a half years and a severe famine spread throughout the whole land. Yet Elijah was not sent to anyone in Israel, but only to a widow living in Zarephath in the territory of Sidon. And there were many people suffering from a dreaded skin disease who lived in Israel during the time of the prophet Elisha; yet not one of them was healed, but only Naaman the Syrian.' When the people in the synagogue heard this, they were filled with anger. They rose up, dragged Jesus out of the town, and took him to the top of the hill on which their town was built. They meant to throw him over the cliff, but he walked through the middle of the crowd and went his way. (Luke 4.14-30)

To Do

The purpose of this exercise is to explore the story in greater depth. Don't be afraid to be really imaginative. We're not trying to pretend that this is historically accurate but to explore empathetically a story which is part of our Christian heritage and which shapes our Christian lives.

Form three equal groups. Each group is allocated a character:

- Jesus;
- a member of the synagogue who was present;
- person with leprosy who heard the story afterwards.

Talk briefly together in each small group about how what happened might have looked and felt to that character.

Then a volunteer from each group should retell the story as that character.

Then ask each other questions to find out how you felt as the characters.

At the end of this activity, it is important for the leader to draw a line under this section and invite people to stop being in character and to be themselves again.

3. Facing Jesus, the image of God (10 minutes)

Jesus is the image of God. We explore why that is such a source of hope for the world, and for us. It might be good to recall here some of what was said in Session 3 about Jesus being the image of God: 'You are my own dear Son. I am pleased with you.' Jesus is also the Spirit-bearer without measure (John 1.34) and the one through whom we receive the Spirit (John 14.16).

To Do

In the whole group: From the story, what can you see about Jesus as the image of God which makes him a source of hope for the world? What do Jesus' actions and words say about God's work in the world which gives us hope?

4. Facing our calling: the image of God as a call and a responsibility (10 minutes)

Jesus calls us as God's people to live in God's image. But people found what Jesus had to say uncomfortable. He makes demands. Growing into the image of God and Jesus involves responsibility, not just privilege.

To Do

How is God calling us to the pain of being 'prophets without honour in our own communities'? (This may include being prophets in our own local churches and denominations.)

5. Facing outwards – an image of hope (10 minutes)

Jesus' message brings hope to the outsiders. 'But the truth is, there were many widows in Israel at the time of Elijah . . . yet Elijah was sent to none of them except to a widow at Zarephath in Sidon.' God has jumped ahead in acting among the marginalized and outsiders of the past like the widow of Zarephath and Naaman the leper. A modern example of similar action is the work of Martin Luther King. Jesus' hearers didn't like what he said, any more than some white Christians liked what Martin Luther King had to say. Did they just want God to be doing things for them? And what about us? How is God calling us to discern what is going on beyond our own boundaries, local and denominational, even beyond the Church as a whole?

To Ponder

Spend a few moments in silence. Think of a person or group of people outside your church community. Ask yourself what the good news of God's salvation would mean for them. You may like to pray for these people when you light candles at the end of the closing worship.

6. Closing worship (20 minutes)

To Pray

For the worship you will need either a table in the centre of the group, or perhaps a cloth on the floor if that is more appropriate.

- After a short silence to gather yourselves for worship, each person in turn places on the central table or cloth the object you have brought to symbolize what you have learned in the group, or what

the group has meant to you. If you feel able to do so, share very briefly with the group why you have chosen this particular object.

- Play some quiet music and reflect silently on what has been brought and said.

- Here are some prayers which you might find useful as you move into a time of spoken prayer. Choose any which are helpful, but feel free to use your own or to have a time of open prayer if you prefer.

> Come, O Lord, in much mercy down into my soul, and take possession and dwell there. A homely mansion, I confess, for so glorious a majesty, but one such as you are fitting up for the reception of you, by holy and fervent desires of your own inspiring.

> Enter then and adorn and make it such as you can inhabit, since it is the work of your hands. Give me your own self, without which, though you were to give me all that you ever had, yet could not my desires be satisfied.

> Let my soul ever seek you, and let me persist in seeking till I have found and I am in full possession of you. Amen

> (St Augustine)

Lord Jesus Christ, let me seek you by desiring you
And let me desire you by seeking you.
Let me find you by loving you,
And love you in finding you.
I confess, Lord, with thanksgiving,
That you have made me in your own image,
So that I can remember you, think of you and love you.
But that image is so worn and blotted out by faults,
And darkened by the smoke of sin,
That it cannot do that for which it was made
Unless you renew it and refashion it.
(St Anselm)

Giver of Life, abide in us, transform us from our former selves into a new life of faithfulness to God's will. Along with all others with whom we live, with all nations and peoples, we would enter a new time, a time of transformation, when hatred is replaced by love, violence by dialogue, condemnation by forgiveness, self-centredness by sharing.

Power of unity, help us to move from the Babel of division to the Pentecost of unity in the diversity of our gifts, traditions and cultures. Make us messengers of the good news, apostles of peace.
(Middle East Council of Churches)

Lord, you are everywhere to be found; never hidden, always present.
We find you in the joy of human friendship,
You sit with us in the security of the family table.
We find you in the depth of Christian fellowship.
You share in the debate and argument that searches for truth;
In reading, writing and the Scriptures' search
In words of prayer and depths of silence.
And best of all, we see you in manger child and questing youth,
In agony and joy,
In obedience and Gethsemane loss.
And miracle beyond our understanding,
You are in me, in him, in her,
In stranger and friend and in age and youth.
Take away the veil that hides you from our eyes.
Forgive the sin that darkens our sight of you.

(Donald Hilton)

Spirit of integrity,
you drive us into the desert
to search out our truth.
Give us clarity to know what is right,
And courage to reject what is strategic;
that we may abandon the false innocence
of failing to choose at all,
but may follow the purposes of Jesus Christ, Amen

(Janet Morley)

You might like to take a tealight or small candle, light it and place it on the table or cloth along with the objects you brought. As you do so, commit to God, out loud or in silence, someone or some situation in need of God's hope. You may like to name the people you thought of at the end of today's discussion.

Leader: But Jesus walked through the middle of the crowd and went his way.

God of love, God of courage, God who calls – you have spoken to us in your word through the story of Jesus your Son, and through the stories of John the Baptist and the ordinary people of Galilee and the Jordan valley. You have made us in your image; you have given us your Spirit. Stay with us in our own Lenten journeys, as we struggle together to learn who we are before you. Give us your love and courage as we seek to learn the stories of others in our world and to speak and live the message of good news – that all flesh may see the salvation of God. Jesus, the image of God, passes through the midst of us; may we follow him on his way. Amen

The image and likeness of God

Section

3

The image of God in the Bible

'The image of God' is a biblical phrase, used in a number of places and a number of ways. Perhaps the most important text comes at the climax of the creation story in Genesis 1.26-28:

Then God said, 'And now we will make human beings; they will be like us and resemble us. They will have power over the fish, the birds, and all animals, domestic and wild, large and small.' So God created human beings, making them to be like himself. He created them male and female, blessed them, and said, 'Have many children, so that your descendants will live all over the earth and bring it under their control. I am putting you in charge of the fish, the birds, and all the wild animals.'

The Good News Bible quoted here says that God created human beings 'like himself', but many other translations say 'in his image and likeness'. This has traditionally been taken to indicate that there is something distinctive about human beings as compared to the rest of creation, and that the distinctive thing is 'the image of God', although what that means has been hotly disputed. Sometimes, particularly in Eastern Orthodoxy, the two terms 'image' and 'likeness' have been seen as referring to different

things, and so the different uses of the words in the list of Adam's descendants in Genesis 5 is seen as significant (note especially verses 1b and 3b). We shall return to this issue in the section 'The Image and Likeness of God'.

When God makes a covenant with Noah, the ban on murder is based on the fact that human beings are made in God's image (Genesis 9.6).

Interestingly, there are no direct references to the image of God in the Old Testament beyond these few chapters at the beginning of Genesis. In the New Testament, the phrase is still used in the same way to indicate the specialness of humanity, as in James's letter (James 3.9).

There is also a new emphasis, however, with Jesus Christ being described several times as 'the image of God', or a similar phrase. Colossians 1.15; 2 Corinthians 4.4; Hebrews 1.3; Philippians 2.6.

The 'image of Jesus' is also found in the New Testament, often as a description of what God's people will be: Romans 8.29; 1 Corinthians 15.49; 2 Corinthians 3.18; Colossians 3.10; 1 John 3.2.

A fall or a failure to climb?

The story of Creation and the 'Fall' is told in chapters 2 and 3 of Genesis. It is one of the best known stories in these islands and is deeply embedded in our literature and culture. Most people, Christian or not, know about Eve and the apple, although they may not realize that the Bible does not name the forbidden fruit. In some cultures it is thought to be a fig. According to Genesis, Adam and Eve were told that they could eat from any tree in the Garden of Eden except the tree of the knowledge of good and evil. Eve was tempted by the serpent, ate the fruit – and so did Adam. As a result they 'fell' from their original innocence. They became exiles, and had to work hard and suffer pain.

Many who know the story reject it as a myth in the fairy story sense and believe that its only relevance to life today is that it has been, and still is, used to oppress women. Among Christians, some still take this story literally. Most Christians, however, are happy to accept the story as a myth in the sense that myths can express deep truths which remain true however much knowledge develops. In this sense the story illuminates the human condition but cannot be harmonized literally with a scientific understanding of the world.

We owe to St Augustine the developed concept of the 'Fall' which for many centuries formed the cornerstone of the Western Christian understanding of the human condition. According to him, God created perfect, ageless human beings, who had control over their bodily passions and lived in perpetual bliss. Eve's disobedience resulted in their loss of innocence and freedom. After the 'Fall' human beings lost the image of God, were tainted by original sin and punished with a life of toil and pain and death. We are born as sinners with a nature that is bound to lead us into further sin. According to St Augustine, we have all inherited not only this sinfulness but also guilt. The stain of sin and guilt can only be washed away by baptism and those who are not baptized are destined for hell. Only by God's grace will human beings eventually be saved (though not, according to this view, all of us).

These doctrines of original sin and the 'Fall' have been controversial among Christians for many years. Those who cannot reconcile St Augustine's view of perfect human beings (who then fell) with a modern scientific understanding of the world still believe that we do have something of the image of God at our birth in the sense that we are able to make moral choices and have the possibility of a relationship with God. We have not so much fallen as failed to climb. Our call is to grow into that image throughout our lives. We will not reach its perfection during our earthly lives, but we can trust in the grace of God and his love as revealed in Christ and look forward with hope.

Image and identity

In preparing this course, we found ourselves talking a lot about identity; so much so that we thought it would be useful to look at how it related to being made in the image of God. 'Identity' describes the things that make us the people we are. This raises the first problem, because the things that are important to who we are may be different from those society tells us are important. For instance, other people might assume that what really matters about me is the school I went to, who my parents were, or the job I do, whereas I might feel that my religious beliefs or my understanding of my sexuality are much more important.

If being made in the image of God is what makes us human, then identity is what makes us the particular human beings we are. Obviously, then, the two are related, but they must also be kept distinct. Some identities, particularly those imposed by society, are very negative ('he's a convicted murderer!' – or, in Jesus' day, 'he's a tax collector; she's a sinner!'); others, even self-adopted, are perceived as negative by certain members of society (racism, sexism, and other forms of discrimination are examples of negative perceptions like this). Given this, if we confuse image and identity we might deny full humanity to certain people.

There is no doubt that this has regularly been done. The writing group spent time listening to people whose gender, sexuality, ethnic origin, or disability had led to them being treated unequally. Their creation in the image of God had been denied, and they felt as if they were being treated as less than human.

How should we relate image and identity, then? Jesus is the true image of God, according to Colossians 1.15. We can say various things about Jesus' identity: he is male; Jewish; a carpenter; and so on. None of these things are part of his being the image of God, but they perhaps point to an important truth: every human being has a particular identity, made up of all sorts of factors. Thus the image of God is not some strange generic humanity, without gender, nationality, and so on. Instead, to be made in the image of God, to be human, necessarily involves having a particular identity. We must say, however, that no identity can destroy the image of God in any human being. Equally, no identity we choose, or that is imposed on us by others, can make us less than human.

Because of the way God has created us, human beings are important and valuable, and nothing can change this.

The image and likeness of God

Genesis 1.26-28 mentions both the image and likeness of God. In the Orthodox tradition these have been distinguished from as far back as the second century. St Irenaeus of Lyon was one of the first to make this distinction. St Cyril of Jerusalem puts it this way:

> At that time, God said, Let us make man after our image and after our likeness. And the image he received but the likeness through his disobedience he obscured.

The 'image' of God in human beings is the potential capacity they have to grow to be more Godlike. Every human being has this capacity, simply by being human. It is not created by the quality of their ethical living. But 'likeness' refers to whatever happens when people try to follow the gospel teaching and to live after the pattern of Jesus' life of love. They gradually come to reflect God's own Trinitarian love in new ways. 'Likeness' therefore refers to the dynamic quality of the Christian life as unending growth.

In the New Testament Jesus is the one who is the perfect image of God, who reflects God's likeness perfectly, both in his own person and in his saving work. In contemplating Jesus, human beings can see the Father's merciful love and compassionate action towards them.

St Diadochos, Bishop of Photiki (c. 400–486), explains his understanding in these words:

> All we human beings are in God's image: to be in his likeness belongs only to those who through much love have subjected their freedom to God . . . Holy grace bestows two good things on us . . . (of these) one . . . needs our co-operation. When indeed the intellect begins to taste the goodness of the All-Holy Spirit with great awareness, then we ought to know that grace is beginning to paint, as it were, the likeness over the image . . . just as portrait painters mark out the outlines of the person in monochrome, then little by little adorning colour by colour, until they capture the appearance of the subject down to each hair. In the same way God's holy grace shapes through baptism the image the human being possessed at his coming into existence, but when it sees us filled with longing and yearning for the beauty of the likeness and standing naked and undaunted in its workshop, it adorns virtue with virtue and leads the soul's form up from glory to glory, preserving for her the impression of the likeness.

Male and female in the image of God

So God created humankind in his image, in the image of God he created them; male and female he created them. (Genesis 1.27)

This verse appears to set female and male, women and men, together as equals in the image of God. But such has not always been the interpretation. At least three interpretations of the significance of this 'male and female' can be found in the Christian tradition. All three are potentially egalitarian; all three have in fact been twisted to make women appear as inferior.

First there is the interpretation which sees the third part of the verse ('male and female he created them') as being connected to the first two parts and as having something to say about the image of God. What it tells us is that women and men together complementarily make up the image of God. Unfortunately this view is distorted by the suggestion that within this joint image men represent the mind, the rational, indeed the more godlike part, whereas women represent the bodily, the lesser part. Man alone may be in the image of God; woman alone may not. This view has had great influence.

Secondly, there is the interpretation that 'male and female' has nothing to do with the image of God. In fact God is beyond gender and beyond sexuality in every way. This view heavily influenced some of the Early Church's emphasis on the importance of virginity and chastity for both men and women. In principle this could be liberating for women, as on this view what sex you are does not matter; all are potentially equal disciples. The sad fact is that in practice this view led to women asserting that by living a virgin life (and only by living a virgin life) they could be equal to men (vir means man in Latin). On this view, men are still the norm; and sexually active women are beyond the pale.

Thirdly, there is the view that 'male and female' refers specifically to the verses which follow, about life on earth as sexual creatures among other creatures who are fruitful and multiply. This again allows for an egalitarian view of the lives of men and women on earth together. In reality, many Christians have argued that God may have created men and women equal before God and in respect of salvation, but here on earth God has rules for the way social life should be ordered and those rules include the submission of women to men. This is what much of the Church still lives and teaches.

Why does this confusion matter? It matters because women all over the world experience poverty and violence because they are women. This also happens in the churches, as a recent report from the World Council of Churches clearly shows. This is a scandal. It is a matter of life and death not a matter of a fad for 'political correctness'. Women have less access to vital resources, and women are violently abused because they are less valued than men. What is godlike is valued; what is considered less than godlike is less valued. There is a connection between the extent to which women are truly seen as being in the image of God and the extent to which they are valued. The theologian Mary Daly wrote that 'if God is male, then the male is God'. Could it be that if, in our Christian communities, we act and speak in ways which associate God more with men than with women (for example in declaring men to be more fit as leaders, teachers and priests, and in regarding male language about God as more appropriate than female language) we are colluding in the increase of women's deprivation and suffering? After all, belief and practice go together. It is encouraging that many Christian communities are looking for creative ways to address these problems – from work on inclusive language to breaking the silence in the churches about domestic abuse.

Excluded from the image

Then have done with falsehood and speak the truth to each other, for we belong to one another as parts of one body. (Ephesians 4.25)

What does it mean to feel excluded from the image of God? Many communities know what it feels like: communities who define themselves or who are defined by their ethnicity, sexuality, disability, religion or by their experience of seeking asylum, for example. They are portrayed as less than human, or a criminal element, a blot on the landscape. They are not often portrayed as 'normal', law abiding, contributing members of their families and the community. Discrimination is an ever present evil that affects the lives of many people, denying them equal opportunities on a level playing field not only in employment and education but also in the Church. Discrimination will never be eradicated until we start speaking the truth and dropping the mask. We have to speak the truth about the lack of equality and drop the mask that says everything is all right in our community and in our churches. Discrimination is a reality. To point this out is not political correctness gone mad nor the imaginative speculations of society's losers or even 'certain' people whining because they like to complain. This condition is a reality, which can have devastating consequences such as racial abuse and violence. We have to enable those who have power to effect change (as well as those who feel they do not) to acknowledge the truth of discrimination in our society.

Rage can bring clarity of mind. When Jesus drove out the money changers from the Temple he demonstrated with forceful clarity that the Temple, far from being a place of worship, had become a place of corruption and oppressive practices that disadvantaged the poor. 'Stop making the house of my father into a marketplace!' (John 2.16). Some people have found that anger, rather than consuming them, can bring clarity to complex issues. Confronting their anger about the Church, for instance, has brought a realization for some Christians that injustice exists there too. Indeed, it is sometimes here that the most denial takes place about discrimination. Good Christian folk often cannot believe how racism and other forms of exclusion can limit the experiences of many within the Church or how they continue to benefit from an unjust institution. To see the reality of discrimination it is necessary to look at the subtle (and sometimes not so subtle) ways in which people are excluded from positions of authority; how they are made invisible in our churches and kept on the margins. Even our spirituality and theology can be tools that maintain the oppressive status quo in many of our churches.

Martin Luther King had a dream of a community united by a concern for equality and true freedom for all. Breaking through our denial is a first step on this shared road of struggle; speaking the truth and dropping the mask. Yet, speaking truthfully about inequality makes demands on us and our institutions. People feel frightened and guilty when they begin to look at these issues. Some (especially those who benefit from the present system) prefer to bury their heads in the sand for fear of being called to account for the extent of discrimination against minority groups around. But, as Scripture says, the truth will set us free, free to discern the ever-present image of God in every member of the Church and society.

Evaluation Sheets

We would appreciate your comments on *Face to Face*. What you say will influence the direction of future Lent study guides. The form should go to: Lent 2004, Evaluation, CTBI, 2 Paris Garden, London SE1 8ND.   Thank you.

First, your group
Our group met in...(house, hall) How many people were there in your group?........................
Which churches (denominations) did they come from?................

In the sections below you will find statements with which you may to some extent agree or disagree. Please circle:

1. if you agree 2. if you have no strong views 3. if you disagree

Shape and style of book	**1**	**2**	**3**
Easy to handle	1	2	3
A pleasant change	1	2	3
Illustrations added value to the written word	1	2	3
Good value for money			
	1	2	3

Session 1			
It was helpful to share faith journeys and talk about our churches.	1	2	3
Discussion based on the Bible reading was helpful.	1	2	3

The quotations focused us on 'being made in the image of God'.	1	2	3
The prayers suggested helped us to worship.	1	2	3
Advice about how to prepare for the next session was clear and persuasive.	1	2	3
This was an interesting and helpful session.	**1**	**2**	**3**

Session 2

It was valuable to think about the groups and communities we belong to.	1	2	3
Discussion based on the Bible reading was helpful.	1	2	3
Jean Vanier's words helped to make the subject more concrete.	1	2	3
Using bricks made of card helped to connect with daily life.	1	2	3
The prayers suggested helped us to worship.	1	2	3
This was an interesting and helpful session.	**1**	**2**	**3**

Session 3

It was illuminating to focus on our hopes, fears and the God of surprises.	1	2	3
Discussion based on the Bible reading was helpful.	1	2	3
Looking at genealogies and thinking of other cultures made us more inclusive.	1	2	3
Advice about how to prepare for the next session was clear and persuasive.	1	2	3
The prayers suggested helped us to worship.	1	2	3
This was an interesting and helpful session.	**1**	**2**	**3**

Session 4

Jim Crace's words about what it might have been like in the desert were challenging.	1	2	3
Discussion based on the Bible reading was helpful.	1	2	3
The broken vessel helped to bring the message home.	1	2	3
Advice about how to prepare for the next session was clear and persuasive.	1	2	3
The prayers suggested helped us to worship.	1	2	3
This was an interesting and helpful session.	**1**	**2**	**3**

Session 5

It was good to focus on worship in the final meeting.	1	2	3
Discussion based on the Bible reading was helpful.	1	2	3
Bringing as object to symbolize what you'd learned was a good way of focusing attention.	1	2	3
Telling the Bible story from three points of view made the discussion more enlightening.	1	2	3
This was an interesting and helpful session.	**1**	**2**	**3**

Any other comments or suggestions? Thank you again.

Members of the Lent 2004 Planning and Writing Group

Ms Zoë Bennett Moore, Director of Postgraduate Studies in Pastoral Theology with Anglia Polytechnic University and the Cambridge Theological Federation; lay member of the Church of England; author of *Feminist Perspectives in Pastoral Theology*.

Ms Katrina Bradley, Administrative Secretary for Church Life/Publications at CTBI; recently completed a theology degree at Heythrop College.

Mr David Carter, Methodist Lay Preacher, formerly a school teacher and now an Associate Lecturer in Religious Studies for the Open University.

Mrs Yvonne Craig, author of *Learning for Life*; formerly National Advisor in Adult Education (Church of England) and before that Tutor in Human Sciences at Wesley College, Bristol (Methodist). Convenor and Editor.

Revd Lorraine Dixon, Chaplain of Chester College of Higher Education; a part-time PhD student at the University of Birmingham researching Black religious history in late eighteenth-century England.

Revd Dr Steve Holmes, Lecturer in Christian Doctrine at King's College, London; member of the leadership team of Ashford Baptist Church (Middlesex); formerly Senior Researcher in Mission and Theology for Bible Society.

Mother Joanna, Orthodox nun working in Paris and Cambridge; has been involved in theological and religious education and spiritual formation; completing a doctorate in early monastic spirituality and co-translating the *Lives of the Orthodox Saints*.

Dr Donald Macaskill, works to promote participation in the Health Service, education and Scottish civic society, with particular responsibility for issues of disability and equality; a member of the Church of Scotland; formerly Vice Principal with the Scottish Churches Open College; author of *Re-discovering Faith*.

Mrs Linsi Simmons, Head of Partnership Development at Bible Society with particular responsibilities for research partnerships; keen interest in the interface of the Church and contemporary spirituality.

Mr Pradip Sudra, Executive Secretary to the Alliance of Asian Christians, a multi-denominational agency; a lay member of the Anglican Church; formerly an evangelist with British Youth for Christ.

Revd Nia Wyn Roberts, Rector of Bala in the Diocese of St Asaph, formerly a religious education school teacher, a social worker and a university tutor.

Staff Consultant: **Revd Jean Mayland**, Co-ordinating Secretary for Church Life, Churches Together in Britain and Ireland.

Acknowledgements

CTBI acknowledges with thanks all the tremendously hard work put into the preparation of this course by the Writing Group. Especial thanks are due to Yvonne Craig, the Moderator of the Writing Group and the Editor of the course. She put in hours of work and brought to the task her rich experience and her imaginative and innovative suggestions. We are greatly in her debt.

The publisher (CTBI) also gratefully acknowledges permission to reproduce copyright material in this publication. Every effort has been made to trace and contact copyright holders. If there are any inadvertent omissions we apologize to those concerned, and will ensure that a suitable acknowledgement is made at the next reprint.

The Scripture quotations contained herein are from The Good News Bible published by the Bible Societies/HarperCollins Publishers Ltd © American Bible Society 1966, 1971, 1987, 1992 and are used with permission.

We are grateful to the following for giving us permission to use material for which they hold copyright:

Session 1

The Archbishops' Council: 'Collect for the First Sunday of Christmas', *Common Worship*, 2000.

The Orion Publishing Group: Werner and Lotte Peltz, *God is No More*, 1963.

Session 2

Continuum International Publishing Group: Jean Vanier, *The Heart of L'Arche: A Spirituality for Every Day*, 1995.

Session 4

Penguin Books: Jim Crace, *Quarantine*.

SPCK for the prayer by Kate McIlhagga, 'God of the heights and depths' from *The SPCK Book of Christian Prayer*

Revd Dr Meg Gilley for her prayer 'We bring to you our hopes', previously unpublished.

Session 5

SCM-Canterbury Press: prayer by St Augustine quoted in J. Kelling (ed.), *The Gift of Prayer*.

Christian Education Movement for the prayer by Donald Hilton, 'Lord you are everywhere to be found', from *Seasons and Celebrations*.

Oxford University Press: prayer by St Anselm cited in G. Appleton (ed.), The *Oxford Book of Prayer*.

Continuum Publishing Group for the prayer by Middle East Council of Churches adapted from
J. Carden (ed.), *A Procession of Prayers*.

SPCK for the 'Spirit of Integrity', from Janet Morley, *All Desires Known*, 1992.

Thanks to **Dr Claire Craig for graphics taken from her PhD thesis which represent a geophysicist's model of the earth and its oceans.**